Dearest Laura ~

May your journey be
marked with love, adventure
and wondrous discoveries.

We love you,
Jodi & Suse

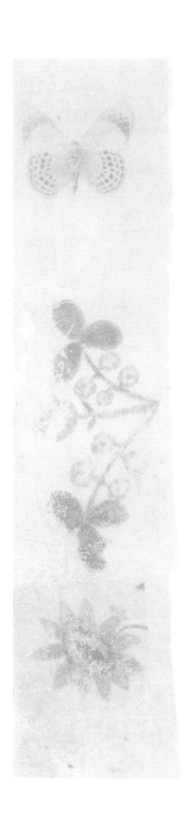

The
New Woman's
Diary

*A Journal for
Women in Search
of Themselves*

Judith
Finlayson

Crown Publishers, Inc.
New York

Published by Crown Publishers, Inc., 201 East 50th Street, New York,
New York 10022. Member of the Crown Publishing Group.
Random House, Inc. New York, Toronto, London, Sydney, Auckland

http://www.randomhouse.com/

Crown is a trademark of Crown Publishers, Inc.

Manufactured in the United States of America

ISBN 0-517-59248-7

10 9 8 7 6 5 4

Contents

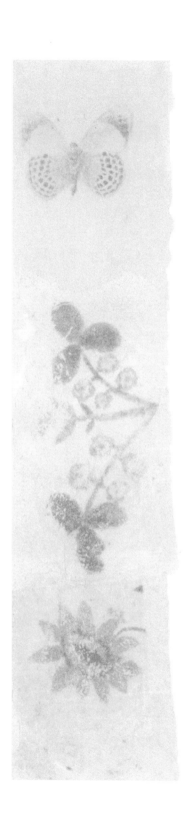

*"We teach what we need to learn
and write what we need
to know."*

—GLORIA STEINEM

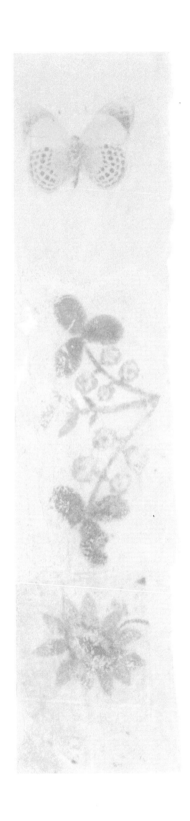

Introduction

I was twenty-eight years old when I began to keep a journal with any regularity, a decision that evolved from personal crises. Not only was my six-year marriage ending in divorce, I had left my career as an editor to pursue a long-standing dream of becoming a writer myself. Nothing was going well, and the spiritual starvation that characterized my life desperately needed to be addressed.

Perhaps not surprisingly, I felt a burning desire to lick my wounds in a safe and private place. So I packed up my car and my two beloved dogs and spent four months in the country, living alone. Nothing in my life had prepared me for such a prolonged period of solitude. Still, some inner wisdom was urging me to pare down and examine my life to see if I could find strengths and feelings to call my own.

In search of this buried self, I filled my car with books by and about women — numerous novels, memoirs, and biographies, as well as a small sampling of literary criticism that was just beginning to chart women writers' search for their own voices. I may not have known it then, but I was looking for connections. I wanted to discover some truths about women's emotions, to see how our lives were reflected in our work and how this information fit with my own experience and what I wanted to do.

Keeping a diary was a natural outgrowth of this

search. Like psychotherapy, writing about experience brings forgotten feelings to the surface where their present relevance can be examined and explored. Basically, the weight of repressed emotions burns up energy and holds us back. Naming these buried feelings frees up energy that can be more productively directed toward understanding ourselves.

Although I didn't know it then, the act of recording and reflecting on my life also initiated me into a long tradition. Throughout history, millions of women, both known and unknown, have recorded their feelings and perceptions between the covers of a book. Their reasons are as varied as the stories of their lives, but perhaps the essence of their quest was captured by novelist Nadine Gordimer when she wrote, "Writing is making sense of life."

Nowadays, women's diaries have become a valid field of study, an especially rewarding vantage point from which to survey the reality of our experience and the connective tissues that unite the female half of the world. The diary is a particularly meaningful form for women, not only because it is one of the few avenues for self-expression that has always been available to us, but also because it balances our lives as society's "invisible sustainers" (to use an expression of the poet and essayist Adrienne Rich).

I think the unacknowledged aspects of women's work — the many hidden "shifts" that define a typical day — help to explain why keeping a diary is especially beneficial for members of the female sex. The most obvious of these is our responsibility for looking after the emotional and physical needs of children, lovers, relatives, and friends — nurturing that can exhaust the nurturer and is often not reciprocated. And, of course, women have seldom mastered the art of nurturing ourselves.

Many women today are consciously trying to move beyond this model, to find new and more fulfilling ways of living that connect us with the active, creative, and spontaneous parts of our being. I'm convinced that keeping a diary can help us in this quest. Having enough faith in our own perceptions to write them down is, on one level, a challenge to the authority that has kept us alienated from ourselves.

When I set out on my inward journey years ago, I sensed, without fully understanding why, that keeping a diary and studying the lives of other women could connect me with my inner self. In many ways I had reached a crossroads. I was becoming aware that most of my education, the study of "great works" written by men, didn't serve me well as a woman. So my search for inner truth was affected by what the German philosopher Nietzsche termed "the art of distrust."

Years later, reading Carolyn Heilbrun's inspiring book *Writing: A Woman's Life*, I came across a thought that seemed to capture the gist of my experience that summer. "Men tend to move on a fairly predictable path to achievement," she wrote. "Women transform themselves only after an awakening. And that awakening is identifiable only in hindsight."

The seeds of my own awakening were sown by solitude and the comfort of books. But my diary provided the fertile soil where they could take root. Buried beneath this nurturing earth, I broke through my conditioning and began my long — and still continuing — journey toward the warm sun of a more authentic self.

Tucked away in my quiet little corner of the world I was also relishing the excitement of discovering a community of women. Reading books that explored a female perspective on the world often touched off the proverbial "click" of recognition. Repeatedly, I felt compelled to capture these insights for future reference, so I began to copy passages from the books I was reading into my diary.

Today we call this process of using books to work through painful situations or to fuel personal growth, "bibliotherapy." Viewing my own experience through the prism of other women's thoughts helped me to see my life differently. It also made me aware of some fundamental truths.

Looking around my study as I write, I feel a deep sense of comfort and companionship. The walls are lined with books by and about women, the vast majority of which have been written in the last twenty years. Mine is not the first generation of women to realize that our past must be discarded because it's more legend than fact. But unlike previous pioneers, we have the skeleton of a documented history, one confirming that many of the problems we experience as individuals reflect aspects of being female in a society defined by men.

Before we can even begin to know ourselves we must cut through a web of assumptions about women — speculations that often carry the authority of fact. The point of embarkation for any journey of self-discovery should be the understanding that what we do, who we believe ourselves to be — even what we feel — reflects our past experience, the expectations of others, and the roles we play in society. Since women have always been the Other, someone who is defined not so much as an individual but rather as a being who exists in relation to men, these aspects of what psychologists sometimes call the "looking glass self" should figure prominently in our quest for authenticity.

A diary is an appropriate place to begin this complex process of self-examination. You will get the most out of your diary if you learn to think of it as a haven where the validity of your experience as a woman can be acknowledged and explored. This theme was prominent in the work of the famous diarist Anaïs Nin, who spoke of building a place of "shelter" in her diary. "The roles that were imposed on me as a woman by my culture I fulfilled….But at the same time, the diary kept my other self alive, it showed what I really wanted, what I really felt, what I really thought."

Joanna Field talks about a similar process of self-discovery in her diary *A Life of One's Own.* She too sensed a dissonance between external reality and her inner self, so she developed a technique to help her bridge the gap. She started to record the best thing that happened to her every day, hoping that this would help her to discover her real needs. The conscious effort to become aware of her own experience kindled many unexpected insights. She began to identify needs that emerged from the core of her being and that were quite different from those she recognized when she didn't stop to observe her life.

I think that diaries are particularly beneficial for women because in many ways their form follows the function of our lives. As Mary Jane Moffat and Charlotte Painter write in their book *Revelations*, diaries are "an analogue to [women's] lives: emotional, fragmentary, inter- rupted, modest, not to be taken seriously, private, restricted, daily trivial, formless, concerned with self, as endless as their tasks."

In the context of contemporary life, "as endless as their tasks" is, perhaps, the aspect of diaries that rings most true. Studies show that women work roughly fifteen hours longer each week than men and that this "leisure gap" is having a devastating effect on our well-being. So not surprisingly, when she studied women's diaries, Lyn Lifshin noticed that "problems with time — structuring it, being overwhelmed by it, a crazy desperateness for more of it — feelings of exhaustion and running" were constant themes. She also found that many diarists expressed concern about "constantly doing things for others" and not doing enough for themselves, of "giving and giving to children, husbands and lovers till there is nothing of self left."

At the very least a diary acts as an antidote, a valuable record of growth that might not be noticed if life is lived in a reactive style, always responding to external demands. The experts tell us that since 1973, the real incomes of average people have been declining and as a result we're running faster and faster just to keep up. When days, months, even years can disappear in the rat race of everyday life, pausing to take a look at ourselves is more essential than ever before.

These are paradoxical times for women. Endless possibilities are offset by encroaching restrictions, which makes it particularly critical that we evaluate how we want to live our lives. We do have choices. The problem is, those choices are rarely as liberating as we wish them to be. And so we must learn to strike a balance, between knowing ourselves and meeting the challenges of daily life, between finding time for ourselves and accomplishing all we need to do in a day.

For centuries we've been lost in a labyrinth of myths about women. Now we must learn to think of ourselves as something of a tabula rasa, a blank tablet. On the one hand, this is an alarming prospect. On the other, the absence of a script is exhilarating because it gives us the freedom to create our own.

One lesson female seekers are learning is that there are no easy answers. Each woman must discover her own individual truths. Even more difficult, perhaps, is accepting this person once you know who she is, since being hard on ourselves is a lesson many of us have learned all too well.

Keeping a diary can help you to become more forgiving, to understand and like yourself more. Make no mistake: the "tomorrow I'll be perfect" syndrome that underlies so many theories of self-improvement is as self-alienating as any of the cultural and religious restrictions that have limited women in the past. Only by learning to live with elements of ourselves that are imperfect can we begin to know ourselves. Accepting these less-than-perfect parts of ourselves is, I think, essential to understanding what it means to be a human being. It is also a starting point for the kind of meaningful growth that keeping a diary can help you to achieve.

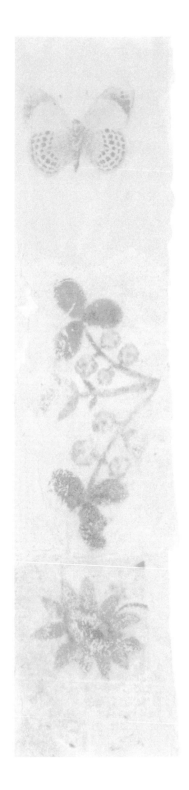

How to Use
This Book

Your diary consists of four basic parts: a working journal, blank pages to reflect on what you have written, a section to record your dreams, and a reading list.

The working section of your journal consists of a series of inquiries into yourself, your relationships, and your feelings. Many of these are enhanced by positive thoughts that can help to get you moving in new directions if you're feeling trapped by old patterns of behavior and emotional response. Quotations from literature build on and expand the process of self-discovery initiated by the investigations. I hope these thoughts will help you see your experience from a fresh perspective and, if appropriate, act as an impetus for change.

As I mentioned earlier, when I began to keep my diary, I found myself entering passages from the books I was reading because I found that other women's insights helped me to see my own experience more clearly. By including quotations that reflect aspects of other women's experience, I have tried to share that process of discovery with you. Use these quotes as a spark, a catalyst that frees your imagination by helping you to move away from the concrete reality of your life.

Possibly, you'll have trouble getting started as a journal writer. Don't be worried. Many people are similarly hesitant. Often it's because they don't know where to begin. For women, these feelings are amplified by the female role. Because our success has traditionally been measured by how well we meet the needs of others, we are likely to mistake self-care for selfishness and experience difficulty focusing on ourselves. The text is specifically designed to help you vault this hurdle and get started as a journal writer.

I hope the words will also get you thinking about some of the broader aspects of being a woman today and how they are reflected in your experience as an individual. But please don't view the text as definitive. As I said, it exists to get you started. There are many different ideas about journal keeping. Once you complete this journal, I hope you will continue on your journey to self-discovery by reading some of the books on journal writing I've recommended in the reading list and developing techniques that work best for you.

Some years ago, I did an *Intensive Journal*® workshop with Dr. Ira Progoff, a psychologist who uses journal keeping as a tool for helping people to see deeper meaning in their lives. Dr. Progoff deliberately encourages participants to make lists of what often seem like mundane details because he believes that the slow, deliberate act of recording the content of our lives gets our creative juices flowing by making us less self-conscious of our search for ultimate meaning. Basically, it's easier to see the larger picture of our lives when we're not aware of looking for it.

In other words, breakthroughs are likely to come when they're least expected. So if you're feeling blocked, have the courage to put your work away. Go for a walk, water the plants, or bake a cake — whatever relaxes you and takes you away from the intensity of creative work. I've long believed that I do my best writing in my sleep. So when I reach an impasse in my work, I've taught myself to put it away, carry on with my day, and have a good night's sleep. In the morning, I usually find that the conditions to create have returned. Or, to use a Taoist saying that Dr. Progoff is fond of quoting, "muddy water, let stand, becomes clear."

Don't feel obligated to do all of the investigations, or to examine all of the issues they raise. As I mentioned, they are really designed to get you started. You will know intuitively which ones are right for you. In fact, you may not see the relevance of a particular investigation until much later in the process of keeping your diary. In that case, return and do it then. And, if an idea has particularly inspired you, don't be restrained by the limitations of this book. Write on loose pages and fold them into this volume (my own journals contain many such notes often written when I felt an overwhelming urge to write and didn't have my journal with me). Or keep a blank book for this purpose.

Your diary also consists of blank pages for *Reflections*. These pages exist so that you can revisit earlier thoughts and feelings. Looking back and reflecting on what you have written is one of the most beneficial aspects of keeping a diary. Moreover, if you read your work carefully, you should begin to see patterns in your life that may reveal areas of weakness requiring change. On the positive side, reading your diary can also help you to identify sources of inner strength.

The *Dream Journal* provides a place to record your significant dreams as a record of self-discovery. Dreams are the language of the unconscious, a dialogue between you and your buried self. Often they contain flashes of insight that allow us to solve problems or alert us to past experiences that we have forgotten. These hidden fragments may have important things to tell us about ourselves, so we are wise to pay attention to what they say.

The final pages of your diary contain a *Reading List* of books that focus on issues of relevance to women today. I have also included some books that explore journal keeping in more depth. This is not an inclusive list by any means. It very much reflects my own biases and often eclectic tastes. But all the books have said something meaningful to me, and I believe they will enhance your own quest for self-discovery.

Before you start to write, spend a few moments trying to create a climate that is conducive to creativity. Sit quietly, experiencing yourself as a physical being. Become aware of your breathing and how your body feels. Make sure you're comfortable and, if possible, relaxed. A quiet place is ideal, where there is nothing to distract you from yourself.

One serious impediment to journal keeping is the fact that women often have no time for ourselves. Diarist Kay Leigh Hagan suggests that one way to move beyond this barrier is to make a date with yourself to write in your journal. Set aside a regular evening. Or take your journal to work. Brown bag your lunch and sit in a park or some other quiet place and write.

Discovering who we are and what we are feeling is usually very empowering. But in the process of keeping your journal you may stir up repressed memories of a particularly painful nature, such as emotional, physical, or sexual abuse. If you begin to sense that parts of your life are missing, are having disturbing dreams, or if some of your memories are just too painful to deal with on your own, please seek professional help.

As you work through your journal, you should begin to feel that your words are building a haven where undiscovered parts of yourself can reside and flourish. Not only is using language to define yourself very self-affirming, in many ways it is a revolutionary act. By laying claim to the power to name and define the world as you see it, you are re-creating yourself while you learn to value who you really are.

PART ONE

Exploring
Myself

It has been said, "If you cannot find it within yourself, where will you go for it?" By helping you to focus on yourself, these thoughts will get you thinking about this new direction.

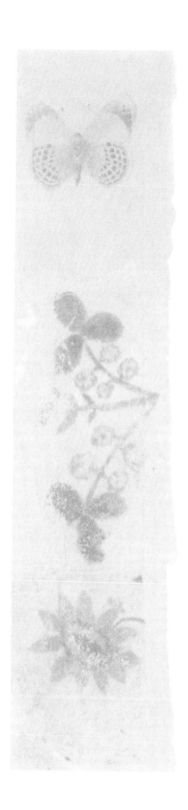

Who Am I?

Putting your feelings about yourself into words can help you to see things about yourself that you might not normally notice. This preliminary sketch of who you are will set the stage for deeper examination as you progress through your journal.

Beginning My Autobiography

In his book *At a Journal Workshop*, Ira Progoff suggests that listing the "stepping-stones" or significant events of our lives is a good way to begin the journal-keeping process. You might want to think of your stepping-stones as chapter headings for a proposed autobiography. Obviously, the chronological events of your life, such as childhood, school days, marriage, etc., qualify as stepping-stones. However, if you have had an emotional experience that looms large in your memory and that initiated a major period of transition—such as the death of a loved one, a painful divorce, violence or abuse, a debilitating failure or an overwhelming success—you may want to identify it as a stepping-stone.

Initially, this "table of contents" will provide you with a capsule look at your life. But after you've worked in your diary for a while, it may also serve as a quick guide to growth. When you revisit this section at a later date, your new self-knowledge may enable you to identify different stepping-stones. If you're so inclined, add these to the list and write about them in the *Reflections* section of your journal.

"The record of a woman's life
written down day by day,
without any attempt at
concealment, as being read, is
always interesting: for I am
certain that I shall be found
sympathetic, and I write down
everything, everything,
everything. Otherwise why
should I write?"

MARIE BASHKIRTSEFF, 1884

My Persona

The "persona" is the part of your personality that represents roles that you play (for instance the devoted wife, self-sacrificing mother, dutiful daughter, superwoman, etc.). Often these function as masks that prevent you from knowing yourself. Creating a third-person description of yourself can help you to identify aspects of your persona that may be impeding your growth.

Write about yourself as you think others see you, or as you would like them to see you. You may want to highlight the achievements that have qualified you to write your autobiography. Let your sense of humor take over, if you're so inclined (for example: as a cum laude graduate of the school of putting others first, she has much firsthand experience of the female role; or as a successful woman she is an expert on how to get ahead in a man's world, often at great cost to herself).

Our sense of ourselves is developed within the context of society's appraisal. This means that if we have been given the message that parts of ourselves are unacceptable, we are likely to keep them hidden. Even so, these buried aspects are very important parts of our being, possibly because we work so hard to keep them concealed. Jung believed, for instance, that if you really wanted to understand someone, you should look for what they tried hardest to hide. Consider this portrait of yourself in this context. Question if you are playing roles to hide parts of yourself that you perceive negatively.

My "public self" is just one small part of me.

> *"On my surface...there must be no sign showing, no seam — a perfect surface."*
>
> <small>HANNAH GREEN, 1964</small>

My Present, Past, and Future Selves

The past, the present, and the future are not separate entities but different locations on a continuous stream. Who we were profoundly affects who we are and who we will be. Looking at yourself from various points in time can provide different "takes" on reality, all of which are yours.

Myself As I Am

The best place to set out on a journey through time is in the here and now. Refer back to your stepping-stones and list the headings that relate to your current life. Then write, "This is where I am. I am…." Give yourself permission to write whatever comes into your mind. Don't edit. Let the ideas emerge freely, one thought flowing into the next.

Now write a profile of yourself, looking more deeply into the characteristics you've identified. For example, I am a lonely person because…. If additional characteristics occur to you, add them. Also consider things such as what you believe in, the kinds of things you do for yourself (for example, having a facial, going for a walk on the beach), why you want to keep a journal, and how you arrived at this decision. Try to include other people's opinions of you, both their criticisms and their praise, and consider how this has influenced who you are. When you've finished, reread your work and reflect on what it reveals about you.

I reflect the people I've known and the experiences I've had. I must
understand my past before I can live my present fully.

*"One's prime is elusive.
You little girls, when you
grow up, must be on the
alert to recognize your
prime at whatever time
of your life it may occur.
You must then live it
to the full."*

MURIEL SPARK, 1961

Myself As I Was

When we find ourselves failing to use our fullest powers, it is often because we have responded to past experiences by developing inhibitions that block our potential. Identifying these blockages can help to make us more self-aware.

Refer back to your stepping-stones and list those relating to your past self. If possible, study some pictures of this younger person and list words or phrases that describe you as you used to be. Write a profile of your former self.

Think about how you have changed, what you have lost, and what you have gained. Thinking about this past self may inspire you to create additional chapter headings for your autobiography (femme fatale? whiz kid? star athlete?). If you've identified new headings, consider whether they represent parts of yourself that you may have buried in response to perceived discomfort, or a blow to your self-esteem. Remember praise or criticism you received and consider how it influenced your feelings about yourself. Once you've finished your profile, you may feel that there are parts of yourself that you would like to reclaim.

If you had happier times, write about them and reflect on why they were so satisfying. Are there ways to introduce these elements into your current life?

Understanding my past will help me to get on with my future.

"Even where the affections are not strongly moved by any superior excellence, the companions of our childhood always possess a certain power over our minds which hardly any later friend can obtain."

MARY SHELLEY, 1818

Myself As I Would Like to Be

Visualizing a positive future is the first step toward achieving it. Listing words or phrases that describe the woman you would like to become may help you to identify your goals and objectives.

Create a profile of your idealized self. In addition to personal qualities consider things such as your financial situation, professional status, who your friends are, and whether or not you have children, lovers, a husband, parents. Expand on your fantasies. Describe your home(s), travel plans, social and romantic life, and what you'd do with your leisure time. Think about what this tells you about yourself.

If there is someone else that you would like to be, you might also want to create a profile of this person. We can learn a lot about ourselves by studying our reactions to others. You might want to think about qualities you admire in other people that you feel you are lacking. Consider what your writing is trying to reveal.

After exploring my daydreams, it became easier to understand
my current needs.

"I see in my imagination a small flat, furnished with exquisite comfort....Beauty everywhere, softness cosiness. And I am the mistress of it — a woman and a personality at the same time. I live an interesting life: writers, artists, painters forgather at my house, a really interesting circle, a close friendly community. I know no picture more attractive than this. I am free, independent."

NELLIE PTASCHKINA 1918

PART TWO

My
Relationships

Our significant relationships are the heart of our inner selves. Parenting figures, siblings, lovers, and friends have influenced the person we've become. Looking at the broad range of your relationships will help to bring divergent aspects of your life together and to expand the scope of your diary work so far.

For this section of your journal consider using one of Ira Progoff's techniques. He suggests creating "dialogues" with persons, events, or things as a tool for facilitating inner awareness.

You can begin your dialogue with a statement from you. For example:

ME: I hate you.

Then have the other respond. For example:

MOTHER: What did I do to hurt you?

Continue until you feel you've exhausted what you wanted to say to this important other.

My Mother/Myself

Our deepest feelings are learned from our parenting figures. Since women are largely responsible for childcare, mothers, in their presence or their absence, profoundly influence daughters' lives. Whether your mother was there for you or not, she has, among other things, deeply affected how you feel about yourself as a woman — your self-esteem, your sexuality, your sense of an independent self. Even if you have consciously chosen to reject your mother as a role model, she flows through your being, often in unexpected ways.

Steeped in the Freudian tradition, we're particularly prone to believing that mother is the source of all that goes wrong in our lives. But mothering doesn't take place in a vacuum. The reality of your mother's life very much reflects historical events, social conditions, and family dynamics. If she failed as a mother, the chances are it's because her own difficulties were overwhelming.

Use this section to explore your feelings for your mother. You might want to think about the ways you see her in yourself, for better and for worse. If you have children, consider how your mother may be influencing your own parenting style. Now that you're an adult, you may be able to recognize some positive things in your mother that your own struggles for independence wouldn't permit.

If your mother wasn't there for you or if she was an extremely negative force, give yourself permission to express your pain. If someone else filled her role, either permanently or on an "as needed" basis, you may want to write about this person as well. Create a dialogue with your mother or her surrogate. Tell her what you have to say and allow her to respond.

"*Tomo even considered taking Etsuko and the money and going back to her home in far-off Kyushu. Yet each time her resolve was weakened by the thought of the future awaiting her daughter, now growing into such a beautiful young woman....If only Tomo herself could bear it, Etsuko would certainly be happier growing up in comfort as the daughter of a man of rank than in poverty in a remote country district of Kyushu.*"

FUMIKO ENCHI, 1957

"To have a mother who loves you for being independent is to have a mother who fosters rebellion in your heart and revolution in your bones."

JUDY CHICAGO, 1975

My Father/Myself

A common theme in the lives of women who achieve public success is their father's blessing. A surprising number of successful women come from families with no male children, and they usually receive a rare degree of support from their fathers, who often treat them like the sons they never had.

The love of a father or a father surrogate is also important to a girl's sense of herself as a woman. To some extent, we search for daddy in every man we meet. If we haven't learned we can count on our fathers, we are likely to become involved with men who aren't there for us or to become "boy crazy" as adolescents. Girls who received the paternal message that sex is bad are likely to have difficulty connecting sex with love. If we were abused by a father, or father surrogate, the breach of trust will have a devastating effect on every aspect of our being.

In this age of all-too-often- absent fathers, it may also be useful to think about the way your father related to his role. Studies have shown that the less time a father spends with his family the more traditionally masculine or feminine the children will be. In other words, a father who is comfortable with nurturing is likely to produce more "liberated" children.

Explore your feelings for your father and how they have influenced the woman you are today. Create a dialogue with your father, saying all the things you've always wanted to say to him and allowing him to respond.

My Lovers/Myself

We choose our lovers for complex reasons. Sometimes they remind us of family figures. Sometimes they're just the opposite. But studying the lovers we choose can teach us a great deal about ourselves.

A lover can be a spouse, or not. But many people believe that sexual desire wanes as commitment grows, and that a spouse soon acquires the patina of a comfortable old shoe. It's also worth considering how the male sense of entitlement often intrudes on heterosexual relationships. When they are involved with men, even the most independent women can find themselves clipping their abilities or putting their own needs on hold.

You might begin this investigation by making a list of your significant lovers. Think about why these relationships were satisfying, or not, and the reasons for your involvement. If you're so inclined, create a portrait of an ideal lover and think about how this person differs from your actual lovers.

You might also want to explore your feelings about your sexuality. Think about your best sexual experiences and whether or not they were part of a loving relationship. Give yourself permission (if it strikes your fancy) to create an erotic vignette starring yourself and think about its message.

"Men write books and
poems about the beauty and
sacredness of motherhood,
but if one looks round the
world one lives in, one finds
that men are, for the most
part, not charmed by the
motherly qualities in women,
and that the women upon
whom men have in the past
lavished titles and jewels
and wealth are not the
motherly type at all."
H. M. SWANWICK, 1913

*"There isn't a woman
alive who is not obsessed
with her sexual desirability.
Not her sexual desire.
Her desirability."*
VIVIAN GORNICK, 1971

"He would come to my house
for dinner. I'll never forget the
flurry of those preparations —
putting flowers in vases,
changing the sheets, thumping
knots out of pillows, trying to
cook, putting on makeup, and
keeping a hairbrush nearby in
case he arrived early. The
agony of it!"
EDNA O'BRIEN, 1967

"She decided that she was too cold a woman to be a mistress and too stubborn to be a wife. She wanted things her way, and compromise held no charm for her; Marianna of the divided heart and soul."

WHITNEY OTTO, 1991

My Family/ Myself

The relationship with our parenting figures is just one facet of our experience as part of a family. It's likely we had (and may continue to have) significant relationships with relatives — not only siblings, but also aunts, uncles, and cousins, not to mention close family friends. When we become adults, we establish families of our own.

Although contemporary families are less and less likely to resemble the nuclear family of the past, responsibility for keeping the home fires burning still rests with women more often than not. Women normally care for children and family members who are old and sick, frequently after a day of paid work. All too often, women fulfill our family obligations at the cost of fulfilling ourselves.

Reflect on what the word *family* means to you, jotting down words or phrases that occur to you. Then develop these ideas into a more fully formed piece. You may want to write about significant family members, past and present. If you have children or a spouse, this might be a good place to explore these relationships.

"*When her biographer says of an Italian woman poet, 'during some years her Muse was intermitted,' we do not wonder at the fact when he casually mentions her ten children.*"

ANNA GARLIN SPENCER, 1912

"A person can run for years
but sooner or later he has to
take a stand in the place
which, for better or worse, he
calls home, do what he can to
change things there."

PAULE MARSHALL, 1969

My Friends/Myself

Only by becoming friends with other women, by understanding what we share — and don't share — can we truly begin to know what it is to be a woman today. Women friends can help us to see through the myths and misconceptions that still characterize our thinking about women today. By nurturing those aspects of our nature that are distinctly female, they can also help us to value the woman in ourselves.

Because men have been more highly valued in our society, we must guard against seeing our women friends as second rate, mere understudies to be cast aside when the male star arrives. Although it's possible to have good male friends, it's worth remembering that male-centered women are vulnerable to not getting their own needs met, for as a rule, it is women, not men, who nurture other women.

Think about your most fulfilling friendships and identify their most valuable aspects. If you have severed relationships with significant friends, or lost them in other ways, reflect on these situations. Consider whether significant elements are now missing from your life and if there's anything you can do to correct this situation.

> *"True friendship is*
> *never serene."*
> MARIE DE RABUTIN
> CHANTAL, 1671

Significant  Others

Moving beyond the private side of our lives represented by lovers, relatives, friends, and family members doesn't make us immune from the influence of others. Far from it, in fact. Teachers, mentors, colleagues, competitors, and so on, can also influence our lives, often dramatically. Nonhumans such as companion animals, particularly those that have been constants in times of transition or stress, can also play major parts in our lives. And even inanimate objects such as books, movies, plays, and works of art can affect how we think and feel. Similarly, significant events such as an accident, a criminal act, or some other act of fate have the potential to change our lives.

Identify some significant others that might have affected your life and write about their importance. If you perceive this "other" as a negative force, make an effort, if possible, to identify the positive fallout from your experience, how it may have helped you to grow.

"All is fish that come to my literary net. Goethe put his sorrow and joys into poems; I turn my adventures into bread and butter."

LOUISA MAY ALCOTT, 1873

My Work/Myself

Today more and more women are able to choose the kind of work we do, whether it is at home or in the paid labor force. Although work can be a source of pride and self-esteem, it is also likely to create conflicts for women. This may reflect the higher value society places on masculine ways of doing things, stereotypes about appropriate female roles, harassment, or the stress of juggling workplace and family demands, among other things. When women work exclusively in the home, the low value society places on homemaking can cause us to have doubts about our self-worth.

Explore your feelings about the kind of work you do, whether you have found work that makes you happy, and how it enhances, or doesn't enhance, your sense of self-esteem. Consider things such as working conditions, the respect and appreciation you receive, the amount of stress associated with your work, and your feelings about success. If you feel that you work too hard, consider whether you're suffering from workaholism, perhaps as a way of avoiding your inner conflicts.

"When a man becomes an author, it is merely a change of employment to him. He takes a portion of that time which has hitherto been devoted to some other pursuit...and another merchant or lawyer or doctor steps into his vacant place and probably does as well as he. But no other can take up the quiet regular duties of the daughter, the wife or the mother....A woman's principal work in life is hardly left to her choice: nor can she drop the domestic charges evolving on her as an individual for the exercise of the most splendid talents that were ever bestowed."

ELIZABETH GASKELL, 1857

"We'll all be better off when word gets around that cleaning a toilet produces no more and no less than a clean toilet; it does not produce strength of character, nor is it interesting work."

GABRIELLE BURTON, 1976

My Body/Myself

The ancient Greeks recognized the link between a healthy body and a healthy mind. Self-esteem — even creativity —is much more likely to flourish when we have a sense of physical well-being. Or, as Simone de Beauvoir reflected, "Not to have confidence in one's body, is to lose confidence in oneself."

And yet, even the most cursory examination of women's history reveals consistent attempts to keep us alienated from our physical and sexual selves, from footbinding and corsets to pornography and myth. Because the influences affecting the way we feel about our physical selves are so complicated, getting in touch with our bodies is, perhaps, a particularly rewarding path of self-discovery.

Begin by exploring some basic issues with your body, possibly in a dialogue. Ask your body if you are caring for it well, providing adequate nutrition, rest, and physical exercise. If your body isn't healthy, explore how you feel about its physical state. Since body image has become a major concern for many women, you might want to consider whether you have bought into oppressive standards of thinness and beauty. These concerns can spill over into other areas of your life, since they can keep you on a treadmill, devoting precious hours and hard-earned dollars to improving how you look.

You might also want to talk to your body about your comfort — or discomfort — with your sexual self. Often it is difficult for us to accept our sexuality as a natural, life-affirming part ourselves.

"Oh it was all so wearying,
so humiliating...had she
really spent so many
years of her life — it
would almost certainly add
up to years! — in front of
a looking glass? Just like
all women. Years spent
asleep, or tranced."

DORIS LESSING, 1973

"I had always despised the body, as the greatest hindrance to all that I most valued. I cannot trace the course when I derived this contempt for the body, but I well remember trying as a child to subdue my body. When going to school in New York I had tried to go without food for days and had tried to sleep on the bare floor."

ELIZABETH BLACKWELL, 1887

My Home/Myself

Our homes reveal a great deal about ourselves. The kind of environment we create for our private space is important to our sense of security, of being nurtured (in the form of comfort), as well as our self-esteem. Striking a balance between a comfortable home and one that makes consuming demands can likely be viewed as an indicator of emotional health. If you are excessively tidy, you may be using housework as an excuse for avoiding yourself. On the other hand if you continually deprive yourself of the comforts of home, you may have difficulty nurturing yourself. Gloria Steinem was in her fifties before she recognized that her disregard for her living space reflected the physical neglect she had experienced as a child.

Because women have traditionally been responsible for "the home," many sentimental homilies have waxed enthusiastic about how much we enjoy domesticity. But all too often, home has not been a safe and happy haven for women. Studies have shown that home is the place where best kept secrets such as battering and sexual abuse are most likely to occur. And meeting the needs of family members has often kept women from finding fulfillment themselves.

Jot down some words or phrases that define what *home* means to you. Develop these into an essay, identifying, if possible, aspects of your home that may be physical manifestations of your inner life. Or you might like to create a dialogue with your home, allowing it to tell you how it feels about your relationship.

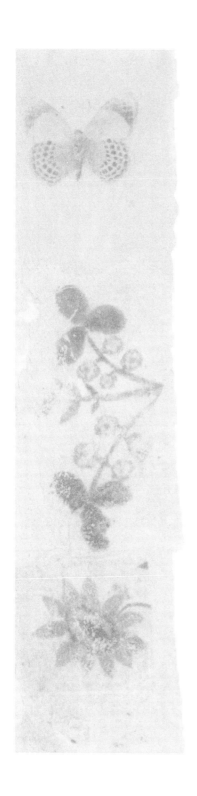

Reflections

PART THREE

My
Feelings

In many ways, feelings are a barometer of truth. How we feel about a person, a situation, ourselves, reveals a reality that reason often obscures. Or as the French philosopher Blaise Pascal once reflected, "The heart has its reasons of which the reason knows nothing."

Like most creative people, Pascal understood that learning to trust our feelings is a step toward healthy growth. Getting in touch with how we feel builds a pipeline to our inner selves.

Even so, we must try to remember that our feelings are not entirely our own. What we feel is solidly rooted in memory. We perceive situations and react to them as a result of our previous experiences in our families and in society. Women in pain are likely to believe that our suffering is our own responsibility, when many of our problems are actually rooted in our status as the second sex.

Feeling Nurtured

Although women are society's nurturers, often we fail to nurture ourselves. Thinking about the things you do for yourself and for others may help you to get in touch with your own needs and become more inwardly attentive.

With our strong "do-gooder" streak it is particularly easy for women to lose ourselves by helping others. There is always something worthwhile that needs to be done, whether raising money for a good cause or making extra work for ourselves to help the environment. The problem is, it's easy to push ourselves to the point of burnout, a vulnerability that all of us share. In her book *Revolution from Within*, Gloria Steinem wrote poignantly about how she drove herself beyond the limit. Comparing herself to a wounded soldier who just kept marching because she was afraid to lie down for fear of dying, she concluded that she never stopped to replenish her inner world because she failed to believe in her own self-vision.

Think about whether you, too, lack faith in your inner world and if you are "soldiering on" because you don't know what else to do. You might also want to reflect on the things that give you pleasure and consider how often you indulge yourself in these experiences. Are you self-nurturing? Or perhaps your problem is just the opposite — you may not be doing enough for other people. In this case, consider whether you have enough outside interests or meaningful relationships to replenish your solitary self.

It's okay to say no and to ask for what I need.

Feeling Guilty

There is probably no such creature as a contemporary woman who is unfamiliar with the experience of guilt. Guilt is a case of "the shoulds," a feeling that has been described as a "struggle between us and ourselves." It's the voice of the controlling parent that we carry within. It is also the voice of a society that places a higher value on men, subtly — and often not so subtly — giving women the message that we don't measure up.

Consequently women feel guilty for all kinds of transgressions: not being caring enough, selfless enough, thin enough, beautiful enough, successful enough, or even being too successful — in other words, for not living up to our idealized image of ourselves. Allowing guilt to get the better of us will erode our self-esteem and may set us up for behavior that makes us feel badly about ourselves.

Think about the things that make you feel guilty. If you're so inclined, create a dialogue with guilt. Talking to your "shoulds" may help you to reject this tyrant in your life.

Allowing stereotypes to dominate my life sets me up to fail. I cannot permit these unrealistic ideals to keep me alienated from myself.

Feeling Used

Women are likely to fall into the role of "givers." We take on too much because being "of use" means we are valuable to others and confirms our sense of self-worth. But when we find that we are constantly doing things for people without receiving anything in return, we are likely to feel "used."

It is humiliating to feel that someone is "using" us, since it denies our value as human beings. When another person exploits our intelligence, concern, love, or sexuality, they are treating us like objects.

All of us have felt "used" at some time. Often it is the better parts of our nature — our desire to reach out, to help, to share — that puts us in this vulnerable position.

Think about times when you have felt used. Examine your motivations for becoming involved in these situations. Don't overlook the possibility that something in your background may be influencing you to do things that may not be in your best interests. Practice saying no.

I am learning to value myself and to identify potential users before
they can exploit my goodwill.

"*To keep anything the way you like it for yourself, you have to have the stomach to ignore — dead and hidden — whatever intrudes.*"

NADINE GORDIMER, 1975

Feeling Like
a Fraud

Having the power to define reality has given men many advantages over women. One of these is the higher value assigned to masculine qualities. This has meant that women often feel that our needs, emotions, physical experience, and perceptions are somehow invalid.

Feelings of fraudulence can haunt even the most successful women. When we "play the game," engaging in behavior that is rewarded by men but that alienates us from our authentic selves, we're likely to feel that we're being dishonest. So, too, when we're praised for traditionally "masculine" achievements such as career success or academic excellence. Because we've received the message that self-enhancing roles are at odds with femininity, whenever we're publicly rewarded we may feel that our success was achieved under false pretenses. On the other hand, some psychologists have also suggested that when women experience feelings of fraudulence in leadership roles it may be a healthy sign — an indication that we may be seeing through the hypocrisy that often underlies hierarchy.

If you've ever felt like a fraud, think about the situations that evoked this feeling. Dreams such as writing an exam you haven't studied for or arriving somewhere naked might be alerting you to these fears. Think about these feelings. Ask yourself if they are warning you that there may be a dissonance between the roles you are required to play and your authentic self.

Being out of touch with myself prevents me from touching others.

"Very few women can be really good at everything they are expected to do....As a result, there is almost always a little failure packaged in with any woman's success in playing her various roles."

ELIZABETH JANEWAY, 1971

"In speech with a man a woman is at a disadvantage — because they speak different languages. She may understand his. Hers he will never speak nor understand. In pity, or from other motives, she must, therefore, stammeringly speak his. He listens and is flattered and thinks he has her mental measure when he has not touched even the fringe of her consciousness."

DOROTHY RICHARDSON, 1938

Feeling Jealous

If you've ever felt the fear of real or imagined infidelity, the dread that comes from realizing that the person you love might find your presence inconvenient or even undesirable, then you've been jealous. If you haven't, then you're probably not being honest with yourself.

Jealousy, which Webster defines as "the fear of being supplanted in the affections of another," is a powerful emotion that can drive normal people to humiliating action. If differs from envy because it is romantic in origin.

Chronic jealously stems from profound insecurity. But if you usually don't feel jealous and you find yourself in a relationship where the green-eyed monster is constantly raising its ugly head, then it might be wise to wonder if your feelings are signaling a hidden truth. Perhaps your lover is unfaithful, or simply unable to make you feel cherished and secure. Your jealousy may be alerting you to the fact that something important is missing from your relationship.

There are few feelings more painful than jealousy. If you are feeling jealous, give yourself permission to pour out your feelings on the page. If jealousy is in your past, take a look at the situations that made you feel jealous and consider what they reveal about you. Habitual jealousy without cause stems from self-doubt, a lack of self-esteem, and feelings of inadequacy. If you were jealous with cause, then you might consider whether you were unconsciously choosing partners who undermined your sense of self-worth.

I must learn to trust my emotions, however painful they may be.

> *"I kept my voice low. I was asking because I was my mother's daughter and I was supposed to be courageous and honest. I didn't want an honest answer. I wished for him to deny everything, or to hand me any contrived explanation."*
>
> MAYA ANGELOU, 1981

Feeling Envious

Envy is resentment of someone who's more beautiful, intelligent, rich, successful — and so on — than you. All of us have been envious at one time or another, and although the emotion is unpleasant, it may have a positive side. Because we envy people who have something that we want, recognizing the sources of envy can help us to identify things that are missing in our lives.

It may be that envy plays a more consuming role in your life. Some people are chronically envious. This is a debilitating sickness that may require professional help.

Consider envy and how it affects your life. Are you chronically envious, or only occasionally so? Perhaps envy is reminding you that you are neglecting important aspects of yourself? You may want to create a portrait of a person whom you envy and consider what it reveals about you. You might also want to compare this with the portrait of your idealized self from part one of this book. Similarities between the two suggest aspects of yourself that require attention.

Being honest about my emotions will teach me things
about myself that can help me to grow.

"Perhaps this was wrong of me, to blame another woman for my own miseries. But that was how I was raised — never to criticize men or the society they ruled, or Confucius, that awful man who made that society. I could blame only other women who were more afraid than I."

AMY TAN, 1991

"One of the troubles with
the word 'insight' as it is
generally used in psychology
is that you really begin to
understand something after
you have begun to change
it....It is only because
women have begun to change
our situation in the world by
ourselves that we can now
perceive of new ways of
understanding ourselves and
our position in the world."
JEAN BAKER MILLER, 1977

Feeling Lonely

There is a big difference between being alone and feeling lonely. We feel lonely when we feel cut off from communication — with others, with our inner selves, and our sources of self-esteem. Moreover, there is no guarantee that surrounding ourselves with people or activities will provide an antidote to loneliness. People can feel lonely in a crowd, within a group of colleagues, or even in their families. The Russian writer Chekhov was making this point when he said, "If you are afraid of loneliness, don't marry."

Ultimately, as philosophers tell us, we are all alone. And yet women do feel lonely when we don't have someone with whom to share our lives. Perhaps because we have been assigned responsibility for relationships, we are likely to interpret the lack of relationship as a blow to our self-esteem.

On another level, women who are consciously seeking a more authentic self may experience the loneliness that comes from being out of step, particularly since society is likely to label us misfits. Until we understand that many other women are equally "misfitted" and seek their company, either in person, or through their writing, painting, or films, we will likely feel threatened.

But here is the paradox. Periods of solitude can be as fulfilling as the most rewarding relationship. And once we recognize these interludes as opportunities for having a relationship with ourselves, we will reap the rewards of this not-so-conventional wisdom.

Constant activity and socializing will not protect me from loneliness,
which shows up when I lose contact with myself.

"It is absurd to suppose that
periods empty of love are
blank pages in a woman's life.
The truth is just the reverse.
What remains to be said about
a passionate love affair? It
can be told in three lines. He
loved me, I loved Him. His
presence obliterated all other
presences. We were happy.
Then He stopped loving me
and I suffered."
COLETTE, 1937

"The solitude (I needed) wasn't a physical solitude....It was an internal solitude that comes about from the fact of being a woman — and a woman with responsibilities in the world of men....Today, I need that kind of solitude so much...that sometimes I feel the need to be physically alone. When I'm with my companion, there are moments when we are two too many. I never get bored when I'm alone, and I get easily bored when I'm with others."

ORIANA FALLACI, 1976

Feeling Anxious

How many works of art define anxiety as a fundamental component of the human condition? Unlike stress, which is a response to external pressures, anxiety is a symptom of inner conflict. This conflict may be rooted in our family relationships — for instance, the difference between the daughter your parents wanted you to be and the woman you've become. Or it may be linked with change and the breakdown of social roles. Today, whether we like it or not, many women are pioneers because we lack role models who have broken the path. This will likely generate conflict as we can't be certain we're heading in the right direction.

Anxiety is the inevitable result of confronting choices that contain uncertainties. But avoidance is no solution. Like turtles, we only make progress when we stick out our necks. Consistently retreating from anxiety results in a limited life, one that is focused on safety rather than satisfaction. But this alienates us from our inner selves. As the Danish philosopher Kierkegaard reflected, "To venture causes anxiety, but not to venture is to lose oneself."

Think about the role that anxiety plays in your life. Are you motivated to expand your experience and grow, or do you retreat from anxiety in unhealthy patterns of behavior? Consider whether you're avoiding situations that make you feel anxious and, as a result, limiting your life.

When I feel anxious, it is because I am trying to grow.

*"Every life decision I have
made — from changing jobs
to changing partners, to
changing homes — has been
taken with trepidation.
I have not ceased being
fearful, but I have ceased to
let fear control me.
I have accepted fear as
a part of life."*

ERICA JONG, 1980

"Mental health, like dandruff, crops up when you least expect it."

ROBIN WORTHINGTON, 1971

Feeling Depressed

In our society, women suffer from a much higher incidence of depression than men, which many researchers believe is due to the self-alienating aspects of the female role. Always putting others first, keeping one's wants and needs down to a minimum, and the kind of approval-gaining behavior associated with femininity have been linked with depression, which has recently been defined as women's "silencing" of ourselves.

Depression is also linked with various kinds of loss: the death of a loved one, physical illness, the ending of a relationship, losing a job, experiencing a blow to our self-esteem — the list is virtually endless. Since women assume responsibility for developing and maintaining relationships, many women, even those with successful careers, are likely to feel depressed if we don't have someone with whom to share our lives.

When we're depressed, the world seems heavy. Even the simplest task can be an overwhelming chore. We feel worthless and certain that our situation will never improve, although it inevitably does. But as with all clouds, there's a silver lining to depression. By slowing us down, depression creates the conditions to help us know ourselves. In fact, depression has often been linked with creativity.

If you're feeling depressed, try to identify your "loss" and to understand it fully. Take control of your negative feelings by writing them down. Pour out your feelings about yourself and your life until you have nothing left to say. Only then will you feel the sense of release and the renewed energy to get on with your life.

When I am feeling depressed I will learn to live life one day at a time
until the black cloud lifts, as I know it will.

"*There is a Langor of the Life*
More imminent than Pain —
'Tis Pain's Successor — When the Soul
Has suffered all it can —

A Drowsiness — diffuses —
A Dimness like a Fog
Envelops Consciousness..."

EMILY DICKINSON, C. 1862

> *"The rules are not created
> for women who want anything
> for themselves; the rules
> are created for women who
> want approval."*
>
> DALMA HEYN, 1992

"If you weren't something,
you shouldn't play act at it.
If you did, you'd have
nobody to blame but
yourself if, one day, the
people for whom you'd been
play acting saw you as
what you had only been
pretending to be."
GAIL GODWIN, 1991

Feeling Angry

How often women have been chastised for expressing anger. It is something "nice" women simply don't do. So instead we hide it away where it festers and grows. The problem is, unexpressed anger eventually becomes resentment, and like all repressed emotions it channels energy away from ourselves.

Throughout history there have always been women who dared to express their anger, but they have inevitably paid a hefty price, inspiring derogatory labels. Even so, it's difficult to deny that confrontation is often the only way to move situations forward. If women are to enlarge the boundaries of our lives, we must become more comfortable with expressing anger.

Perhaps female anger is so dreaded precisely because it is justified, a natural response to the self-effacement associated with the female role. Learning from anger means that we must try to view it as a positive emotion that may be alerting us to missing links, particularly in our relationships. By identifying and confronting the sources of our anger we can increase our knowledge about ourselves.

So give yourself permission to be angry — at your lover, your family, your boss. Pour out your feelings on the page. Learn to have faith in your anger, to think of it as a guide that is leading you toward your true self.

I will not allow fears of being labeled "unfeminine" to prevent me from getting in touch with my anger.

"At first it seemed to me that the problem of the second shift was hers. But I came to realize that those husbands who helped very little at home were often indirectly just as deeply affected as their wives by the need to do that work, through the resentment their wives felt toward them, and through their need to steel themselves against that resentment."

ARLIE HOCHSCHILD, 1989

Feeling Interested

Given that women have learned that others come first, pursuing our own interests has been difficult. We are likely to equate the pleasure that interest brings with selfishness. But without interest, people lack motivation to navigate the demanding road toward self-fulfillment. Interest helps us to enjoy learning. It motivates us to stick with activities until we develop skills and competence. It has often been said that excellence in any field is far less a matter of inspiration than perspiration. By keeping us going the extra distance interest helps us to achieve our dreams and goals.

Interest also keeps us connected with our creativity by making us open and receptive to change. It motivates us to expand our experience and overcome anxiety so we can grow. Without interest, existence would be a kind of death in life. So not surprisingly, loss of interest is a key symptom of depression.

You might want to jot down a list of things that interest you and to think about the role that they have played in your life. Have you found your interests, be they gardening, cooking, music — whatever — inherently satisfying? If so, why? Have they led you in new directions in your work or your social life? Have they helped you to grow? Is it possible that you need to develop some new interests to help you move beyond your current situation? Or perhaps you need to pursue your own interests more.

Healthy involvement in things outside myself can help me to
develop tools I need to fulfill my potential.

"If I can get on my sofa and occupy myself for four hours at intervals through the day, scribbling my notes and able to read the books that belong to me in that they clarify the density and shape the formless mass within, life seems inconceivably rich."

ALICE JAMES, 1890

Feeling Proud

The notion of pride is full of contradictions. On the one hand, it is one of the seven deadly sins, associated with arrogance that causes people to lose touch with themselves. On the other, pride is linked with self-esteem, self-respect, and self-confidence, which are key components of mental health.

We associate pride with our public selves, with status and the pleasure we take in achievements such as career success. Men have traditionally pursued pride directly through award-seeking behavior, but women have been encouraged to experience pride vicariously through the achievements of others, in particular, husbands and children. The low value traditionally assigned to so-called women's work, the objectification of our bodies, and the proliferation of pornographic images that demean women have interfered with our access to pride, which can act as an antidote to the self-negation that underlies the female role.

It is important for women to feel that we have the respect and admiration of others, particularly since that has been so often lacking in our lives. But pride should not be fed completely by external sources. We must also practice valuing ourselves.

Examine the sources of pride in your life and assess whether they are appropriately balanced between the public and the private world. Visualize pride as the goddess within you: strong, self-confident, honest, and true. Imagine how she looks, feels, and how others perceive her. Imagine how you can make these elements part of your life.

I have a right to feel proud of my achievements and to expect
that others will acknowledge my value.

"[Charlotte Brontë] once told her sisters that they were wrong — even morally wrong — in making their heroines beautiful as a matter of course. [When] they replied that it was impossible to make a heroine interesting on any other terms, her answer was 'I will prove to you that you are wrong. I will show you a heroine as small and as plain as myself who shall be as interesting as any of yours.' Hence Jane Eyre."

HARRIET MARTINEAU, 1877

Feeling Powerful

In the process of discovering why women have feared power, we are learning valuable lessons about ourselves. Power, as men have exercised it, is based on hierarchy and dominating others. This goes against women's more relational and consensus-building style.

But in its purest sense power is a creative force, the ability to produce a change. We feel powerful when the material conditions of our lives permit choices and allow us to take care of our own needs or when we can foster the development of others. And, most of all, when we are in touch with our inner selves.

Women's alienation from power is a subject of intense scrutiny. However, psychotherapist Jean Baker Miller believes that our traditional position of weakness may turn out to be women's greatest strength. She's convinced that our ability to deal with feelings of powerlessness connects us more closely than men with the human condition.

Consider your own feelings about power, both as a positive and a negative force. Have you avoided power and paid a price? Perhaps you've bought into a model of power that is causing you to experience discomfort. You may want to create a dialogue with power to help you understand some of the complex feelings it evokes.

My need for power is valid and it is my responsibility to seek ways of
negotiating power that fit with my feelings about myself.

*"Women understand —
only women altogether —
what a dreary will-o'-the-
wisp is this old, common, I
had almost said
commonplace, experience,
"When the fall sewing is
done," "When the baby can
walk,"..."When I am a little
stronger," then I will write
the poem, or learn the
language, or study the
great charity, or master the
symphony: Then I will act,
dare, dream, become."*
ELIZABETH STUART LYON
PHELPS, 1877

*"You have to choose the voice
you are going to trust. You
can't listen to everyone."*

ALICE HOFFMAN, 1992

"The problem is not merely one of Woman and Career, Woman and the Home, Woman and Independence. It is more basically: how to remain whole in the midst of the distractions of life; how to remain balanced, no matter what centrifugal forces tend to pull one off centre; how to remain strong, no matter what shocks come in at the periphery and tend to crack the hub of the wheel."

ANNE MORROW LINDBERGH, 1955

Feeling Joyous

"Nobody knows how little it takes to make me happy" reflected the French writer Colette, defining an essential component of joy. It is something that emerges from within, a kind of spiritual saturation or inner contentment that comes from fulfilling our potential.

Joy can come from different sources at different times. Falling in love, creating good work, a simple walk in the country, all can make our spirits soar. Often, as Colette implied, it is found in the simplest of things. Basically, joy is the capacity to appreciate life.

Think about moments of great joy you have experienced. Are you aware of a sense of heightened reality? Concentrate on the sensual aspects of your experience, the colors of your surroundings, the texture of the materials, the quality of light, and the smell of the air. If joy is missing from your present life, think about why that is so. Is there any way you can change your situation? Contemplate possible alternatives. If you are unable to move beyond your current circumstances, talk about your feelings with a friend.

I am part of a process, a community of women. As we move beyond the old social norms with our new visions and support systems, we will experience the joy that comes from being seekers.

> "Most beautiful of things I
> leave is sunlight;
> then come glazing stars and
> the moon's face;
> then ripe cucumbers and
> apples and pears."
>
> PRAXILLA, C. 450 B.C.

*"It is a glorious wild
solitude under that lofty
purple crag. It stood upright
by itself, its own self and
shadows below, one mass —
all else was sunshine."*

DOROTHY WORDSWORTH,
1802

"'How lovely the air is
here.'...The phrase repeated
itself again and again,
going with her up the
platform toward the group
of lights. It was all she
could summon to meet
the new situation. It
satisfied her; it made her
happy. It was enough;
but no one would think it
was enough."

DOROTHY RICHARDSON,

1938

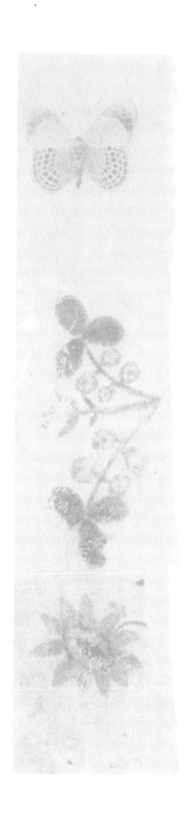

Reflections

Dream Journal

Dreams are messages that emerge from deep inside us, a bridge between our conscious and unconscious selves. They are the language our unconscious uses to alert us to buried aspects of our personalities.

This dream journal is a place to record your dreams during this important period of growth. Document them by date and refer back to your entries to see what they reveal about your progress toward self-awareness.

Reading List

Fiction

Margaret Atwood, *Wilderness Tips*. Doubleday & Co. Inc., Garden City, N.Y., 1991. Any of this writer's novels or short stories can be expected to deliver telling insights into the nature of relationships between men and women. This collection of short stories is particularly sumptuous.

Jane Austen, *Pride and Prejudice*. Penguin Books, Middlesex, England, 1972. A wicked comedy of manners that shouldn't be taken at face value, since Jane Austen was one of the first writers fully to understand how social, political, and economic realities shape consciousness. She used the romance form as a vehicle for her revolutionary ideas about the restrictions that shape women's lives.

Charlotte Brontë, *Jane Eyre*. The Penguin English Library, London, 1966. A rare study of one woman's successful struggle for authenticity in a particularly repressive world.

Colette, *The Collected Stories of Colette*. Farrar, Straus & Giroux, New York, 1983. Deeply sensual, Colette's ability to capture the physical world and the depth of passion in life is unsurpassed. Read her stories to experience their amazing thirst for life.

Fanny Flagg, *Fried Green Tomatoes at the Whistle Stop Cafe*. McGraw-Hill Book Company, New York, 1987. Far better than the movie, this often hilarious yet moving novel about people who don't conform to social norms will make you laugh and cry and will restore your faith in the human spirit.

Marilyn French, *The Women's Room*. Summit Books, New York, 1977. This first "big" novel of the second wave of feminism brilliantly documents the conditions that caused women as a group to question their position in society.

Doris Lessing, *The Golden Notebook*. Michael Joseph, London, 1962. This rather bleak novel broke new ground by introducing us to Anna Wulf, a heroine who is particularly interesting because she believes herself to be gifted. Worth reading not only for its insights into one woman's emotional life but also because Anna keeps journals in which she documents various aspects of her life.

Alice Munro, *Friend of My Youth*. McClelland & Stewart, Toronto, 1990. A collection of beautifully written short stories that reflect the deep undercurrents and magic in ordinary lives.

Whitney Otto, *How to Make an American Quilt*. Villard Books, New York, 1991. An elegantly written novel about a community of women that meets regularly to stitch a quilt, and the underlying connections in their lives.

Jean Rhys, *The Wide Sargasso Sea*. Andre Deutsch, London, 1966. Like all of Rhys's writing, this novel captures the emotional reality of women without power. An imaginative re-creation of the story of the mad Mrs. Rochester in *Jane Eyre*, it's a vivid tale of one woman's "silencing."

Amy Tan, *The Kitchen God's Wife*. G. P. Putnams, New York, 1991. A particularly engaging tale about a woman coming to terms with her mother's life.

Alice Walker, *The Temple of My Familiar*. Pocket Books, New York, 1990. A gorgeously written book about the power to tell our own stories, the value of dreams, and the quest for authenticity.

Nonfiction

Louise Bernikow, *Among Women*. Harmony Books, New York, 1980. A fascinating piece of literary scholarship that examines women's relationships with one another.

Rachel M. Brownstein, *Becoming a Heroine, Reading About Women in Novels*. Penguin Books, New York, 1984. A provocative look at the ways that novels have shaped female consciousness.

Paula J. Caplan, *The Myth of Women's Masochism*. E. P. Dutton, New York, 1985. This book debunks the Freudian theory that women are inherently masochistic and instead presents alternative explanations for behavior that doesn't conform to masculine norms.

Judy Chicago, *Through the Flower: My Struggles as a Woman Artist*. Doubleday & Co. Inc., Garden City, New York, 1975. A powerful story of a woman's struggle to define herself as an artist without denying her sense of herself as a woman. Fascinating for its insights into the early life of the creator of the momentous sculpture *The Dinner Party*.

Luise Eichenbaum and Susie Orbach, *What Do Women Want: Exploding the Myth of Dependency*. Coward-McCann, New York, 1983. A book that turns traditional theories about women and independence upside down, showing how women are *depended upon* and that men are actually the more dependent sex.

Marilyn French, *Beyond Power: On Women, Men and Morals*. Summit Books, New York, 1985. A wide-ranging book that documents the nature and effect of power as we have known it and argues for a new morality based on more human values.

Carol Gilligan, *In a Different Voice*. Harvard University Press, Cambridge, Mass., 1982. A ground-breaking book that examines how women's patterns of development differ from men's and how this has affected our sense of morality.

Carol Gilligan, Nona P. Lyons, and Trudy J. Hanmer, *Making Connections: The Relational Worlds of Adolescent Girls at Emma Willard School*. Harvard University Press, Cambridge, Mass., 1990. A thought-provoking study of how female self-esteem is undermined by adolescence. Certain to evoke "clicks" in every woman.

Carolyn G. Heilbrun, *Reinventing Womanhood*. W. W. Norton & Company, New York, 1979. An enriching look at how women can achieve without sacrificing ourselves.

Carolyn G. Heilbrun, *Writing, A Woman's Life*. Ballantine Books, New York, 1989. A beautifully written book about women writers and their quest for independence that explores possibilities for all women.

Judith Lewis Herman, M.D., *Trauma and Recovery: The Aftermath of Violence — From Domestic Abuse to Political Terror*. Basic Books, New York, 1992. Establishing the connections between the domestic experiences of men in war and women who are victims of sexual and traumatic violence, this book legitimizes the study of trauma as a life-destroying part of ordinary human experience. A healing book.

Dalma Heyn, *The Erotic Silence of the American Wife*. Turtle Bay Books, New York, 1992. A fascinating look at the state of marriage today. Despite initial doubts about their decision, the subjects found that an extramarital affair restored a sense of themselves they had lost in marriage.

Arlie Hochschild, *The Second Shift: Working Parents and the Revolution at Home*. Viking, New York, 1989. A look at contemporary society and the state of relations between men and women through the eyes of two-career parents.

Dana Crawley Jack, *Silencing the Self: Women and Depression*. Harvard University Press, Cambridge, Mass., 1991. A brilliant analysis of the sources of women's depression. Jack argues that women "silence" themselves and sacrifice their own needs in order to preserve relationships, and that this loss of self causes depression.

Elizabeth Janeway, *Man's World, Woman's Place: A Study in Social Mythology*. William Morrow, New York, 1971. A fascinating and scholarly book about the ways that myth develops to justify forms of social organization, in this case women's secondary status. A classic.

Judith V. Jordan, Alexandra G. Kaplan, Jean Baker Miller, Irene P. Stiver, Janet L. Surrey, *Women's Growth in Connection: Writings from the Stone Center*. The Guilford Press, New York, 1991. The work done at the Stone Center has transformed how we think about women. This collection of some of the significant papers to emerge from this "think tank" covers many topics that will interest women who are questioning their place in the world.

Harriet Goldhor Lerner, *The Dance of Anger: A Woman's Guide to Changing the Patterns of Intimate Relationships*. Harper & Row, New York, 1985. An often insightful book that provides direction in transforming anger into a constructive force.

Anne Morrow Lindbergh, *Gift from The Sea*. Vintage Books, New York, 1991. Written in the fifties and embellished with an afterword when it was reissued in 1975, this gentle book has an appealing quaintness that reflects its age. Even so, there is much wisdom in these meditations on youth and age, love and marriage, solitude, peace, and contentment.

Rollo May, *The Courage to Create*. W. W. Norton & Company, New York, 1975. A book that questions the nature of creativity and concludes that the power to create exists within all of us waiting to be tapped.

Jean Baker Miller, *Toward a New Psychology of Women*. Beacon Press, Boston, 1977. A milestone in our understanding of female psychology, this small book looks at women's quest for authenticity within the context of meeting others' needs and concludes that women's way of living may have far more to offer the world than traditional wisdom suggests.

Tillie Olsen, *Silences*. Delacorte Press, New York, 1978. A moving account of the various impediments that have "silenced" artists throughout history, including Olsen herself, who found that the demands of supporting and caring for children prevented her from fulfilling her creativity. A brave and thoughtful book.

Adrienne Rich, *Of Woman Born: Mother-hood as Experience and Institution*. W. W. Norton, New York, 1976. A richly documented examination of motherhood that combines the author's personal experience with historical analysis. An inspiring writer tackles an important subject.

Adrienne Rich, *On Lies, Secrets and Silence: Selected Prose, 1966–1978*. W. W. Norton, New York, 1979. Although many of these essays were written almost two decades ago, their clarity and eloquence make them valuable today.

Gloria Steinem, *Revolution from Within*. Little Brown, Boston, 1992. A thoughtful book examining why women's search for self-esteem encounters so many obstacles.

Anthony Storr, *Solitude: A Return to the Self*. Flamingo, London, 1989. An examination of the virtues of solitude by an eminent psychiatrist.

Naomi Wolf, *The Beauty Myth*. Random House Canada, Toronto, 1990. An exposé of the "beauty myth," the ways that oppressive standards of appearance function as a political tool for holding women back.

Virginia Woolf, *A Room of One's Own*. The Hogarth Press, London, 1929. This classic discussion on why we have no female Shakespeare is an engaging analysis of the female condition, especially worth reading for what it reveals about women's awareness of sexual politics half a century ago.

Letters and Diaries

Fanny Burney, *Selected Letters and Journals*, ed. by Joyce Hemlow. Clarendon Press, Oxford, 1986. Called "the mother of the English novel," Fanny Burney used the proceeds of her pen to support her husband and their child. This selection of her diaries, which opens in 1793, offers a fascinating account of history from a woman's perspective and provides a unique sourcebook on the reality of women's lives.

Emily Carr, *Hundreds and Thousands*. Clarke Irwin, Toronto, 1966. These delightful diaries of a brilliant artist whom many would consider eccentric are full of wise observations about life and the meaning of art, the value of solitude, and the experience of joy.

Colette, *Letters from Colette*. Ballantine Books, New York, 1983. She has been called "the greatest of French women writers." The private side of this remarkable woman strengthens our sense of her as a woman with a gigantic appetite for life.

Isak Dinesen, *Letters from Africa*. The University of Chicago Press, 1981. A vivid collection of letters, written by the author of *Out of Africa*, that provides fascinating insights into her inner life. The editor called them "messages of hope...particularly for women but for all lonely freethinkers."

Lyn Lifshin, ed., *Ariadne's Thread, A Collection of Contemporary Women's Journals*. Harper & Row, New York, 1982. A wide-ranging collection of journals that provides a unique look into the thoughts and feelings of contemporary women.

Katherine Mansfield, *Letters and Journals*, ed. by C. K. Stead. Penguin Books, New York, 1977. Although Katherine Mansfield was only thirty-four when she died, she left behind some of the most finely crafted short stories in the English language. Her private writing reveals the mind of a gifted writer at work, among other things.

Mary Jane Moffat and Charlotte Painter, eds., *Revelations: Diaries of Women*. Vintage Books, New York, 1975. Selections from women's diaries, interesting for the wide range of experience they capture as well as their insights into the inner lives of women.

Anaïs Nin, *The Diary of Anaïs Nin*, ed. by Gunther Stuhlmann. The Swallow Press and Harcourt, Brace and World, New York, 1966. Although they have been criticized for Nin's inability to transcend feminine narcissism, her diaries deserve to be read as groundbreakers that explore the diary as a medium for self-discovery.

Jean Rhys, *Letters, 1931–66*, ed. by Francis Wyndham and Diana Melly. Penguin, Harmodnsworth, 1985. Although she published several brilliant novels early in her career, Jean Rhys lived most of her life in obscurity. With the publication of *The Wide Sargasso Sea* in 1966 her true worth as a writer was recognized. These letters offer a rare glimpse into a life of constant struggle against poverty, depression, and what we would likely diagnose today as chronic fatigue syndrome. Even so, her letters often reveal humor and the determination that resulted in her eventual triumph.

Hannah Senesh, *Her Life and Diary*. Schocken Books, New York, 1971. Hannah Senesh was a Hungarian who devoted her young life to helping other Jews escape from occupied countries. She was tortured and executed by the Nazis when she was 23 years old. Her diary is a testament to moral courage and the triumph of the human spirit.

Virginia Woolf, *The Diary of Virginia Woolf*. Harcourt, Brace and Jovanovich, New York, 1977 and following. These diaries provide us with a fascinating slice of literary gossip and history, and were the private place where Woolf unburdened her doubts and fears about herself and how her writing would be received.

Journal Keeping

Christina Baldwin, *One to One, Self-Understanding Through Journal Writing*. M. Evans & Company, New York, 1977. An examination of the diary's potential to facilitate personal growth, this small volume combines a personal story with practical tips for enhancing the value of the journal-keeping process.

Joanna Field, *A Life of One's Own*. J. P. Tarcher, Los Angeles, 1981. A woman's reflections on what keeping a journal taught her about the meaning of her life.

Kay Leigh Hagan, *Internal Affairs, A Journal-Keeping Workbook for Self-Intimacy*. Harper & Row, San Francisco, 1990. A "hands-on" guide to using the journal for self-actualization.

Ira Progoff, *At a Journal Workshop*. Dialogue House Library, New York, 1977. The basic textbook for using the Intensive Journal® process developed by Dr. Progoff.

Tristine Rainer, *The New Diary*. J. P. Tarcher, Los Angeles, 1978. A "how-to" book on maximizing the value of journal keeping as a tool for self-discovery.

Acknowledgments

Quotations have been taken from the following sources.

Alcott, Louisa May. *Louisa May Alcott: Her Life, Letters and Journals*, ed. Ednah D. Cheyney. Robert Brothers, Boston, 1889.

Angelou, Maya. *The Heart of a Woman*. Random House, New York, 1981. Used by permission of Random House.

Barrett, Elizabeth. *The Barretts at Hope End: The Early Diary of Elizabeth Barrett Browning*, ed. Elizabeth Berridge. John Murray, London, 1974.

Bashkirtseff, Marie. *Marie Bashkirtseff: The Journal of a Young Artist*, trans. by Mary J. Serrano. E. P. Dutton and Co., New York, 1923.

Behar, Joy. Quoted in an interview with Regina Barreca in *They Used to Call Me Snow White But I Drifted*. Penguin Books, New York, 1991.

Bernhard, Sandra. Quoted in "The Divine Sandra," by Jesse Green. *Mirabella*, August 1992.

Blackwell, Elizabeth. Letter to her daughter, Kitty, in *Between Ourselves: Letters Between Mothers and Daughters*, ed. by Karen Payne. Houghton Mifflin Company, Boston, 1983.

Brontë, Charlotte. *Jane Eyre*. Penguin Books, Middlesex, England, 1966.

Brownmiller, Susan. *Femininity*. Linden Press/Simon & Schuster, New York, 1984. Copyright © 1983 by Susan Brownmiller, reprinted by permission of Simon & Schuster, Inc.

Burton, Gabrielle. To the Symposium on Women's Health, 1976. Quoted in *They Used to Call Me Snow White But I Drifted*, by Regina Barreca. Penguin Books, New York, 1991.

Chicago, Judy. *Through the Flower: My Struggle As a Woman Artist*. Doubleday & Co. Inc., Garden City, New York, 1975. Used by permission of the author.

Child, Lydia. *Letters from New York*. C. S. Francis & Co., New York, 1852.

Colette, excerpt from "Bella Vista" from *The Collected Stories of Colette*. Farrar, Straus & Giroux, Inc., New York, 1983. Translation copyright © 1983 by Farrar, Straus & Giroux, Inc. Reprinted by permission of Farrar, Straus & Giroux Inc., and Martin Secker and Warburg Ltd.

Davis, Rebecca Harding. From *Life in the Iron Mills*, quoted in *Silences* by Tillie Olsen. Delacorte Press, New York, 1978.

Dickinson, Emily. *Emily Dickinson's Poems*, selected and introduced by Thomas A. Johnson. Little, Brown, Boston, 1960.

Dodge, Mary Mapes. *Hans Brinker or The Silver Skates, A Story of Life in Holland*. Scribner's, New York, 1899.

Eliot, George. *The Mill on the Floss*. Routledge, London, 1991.

Enchi, Fumiko. From *The Waiting Years*, trans. by John Bester. Kodansha International, Ltd., New York, 1971. Copyright © 1971 by Kodansha International, Ltd. Reprinted by permission. All rights reserved.

Fallaci, Oriana. "The Art of Unclothing an Emperor," in *Forever Young*, by Jonathan Cott. Random House, New York, 1977. Used by permission of Random House, Inc.

Gaskell, Elizabeth. *Life of Charlotte Brontë*. D. Appleton, New York, 1857.

Godwin, Gail. *Father Melancholy's Daughter*. William Morrow and Co., New York, 1988. Copyright © 1988 by Gail Godwin. Used by permission of William Morrow and Co., Inc.

Gordimer, Nadine. *The Conservationist*. Jonathan Cape, London, 1974. Copyright © 1972, 1973, 1974 by Nadine Gordimer. Used by permission of Jonathan Cape and Viking Penguin, a division of Penguin Books, U.S.A., Inc.

Gornick, Vivian. From "Woman as Outsider" in *Woman in Sexist Society, Studies in Power and Powerlessness*, ed. by Vivian Gornick and Barbara K. Moran. Copyright © 1971 by Basic Books, Inc. Reprinted by permission of Basic Books, a division of HarperCollins Publishers.

Green, Hannah. *I Never Promised You a Rose Garden*. Holt, Rhinehart and Winston, New York, 1964. Used by permission of Henry Holt and Company Inc.

Harrison, Barbara Grizzuti. From "Dorothy Sayers: Feminism and Individuality" in *Off Center*. Doubleday, a division of Bantam Doubleday Dell Publishing Group, Inc., New York, 1980. Copyright © 1980 by Barbara Grizzuti Harrison. Used by permission of Doubleday, a division of Bantam Doubleday Dell Publishing Group, Inc.

Heilbrun, Carolyn. *Writing: A Woman's Life*. W. W. Norton, New York, 1988. Used by permission of W. W. Norton and Company.

Hellman, Lillian. *Pentimento*. Copyright © 1973 by Lillian Hellman. By permission of Little, Brown, and Company.

Heyn, Dalma. *The Erotic Silence of the American Wife*. Turtle Bay Books, New York, 1992. Used by permission of Random House, Inc.

Hochschild, Arlie, with Anne Machung. *The Second Shift: Working Parents and the Revolution at Home*. Viking Penguin, a division of Penguin Books U.S.A., Inc., New York, 1989. Copyright © 1989 by Arlie Hochschild. Used by permission of Viking Penguin, a division of Penguin Books, U.S.A., Inc.

Hoffman, Alice. Quoted in an interview in the *New York Times*, May 21, 1992.

James, Alice. Quoted in *Alice James, A Biography* by Jean Strouse, Houghton Mifflin Company, Boston, 1980.

Janeway, Elizabeth. *Man's World, Woman's Place: A Study in Social Mythology*. Copyright © 1971 by Elizabeth Janeway. Used by permission of William Morrow & Company, Inc.

Jong, Erica. "Blood and Guts: The Tricky Problem of Being a Woman Writer in the Late Twentieth Century" in *The Writer and Her Work, Contemporary Women Reflect on Their Art and Situation*. Edited with an introduction by Janet Sternburg.

W. W. Norton and Company, New York, 1980. Copyright © 1980 by Erica Jong. Reprinted by permission of Sterling Lord Literistic, Inc.

Laurence, Margaret. *A Jest of God*. McClelland and Stewart, Toronto, 1989. Used by permission of the author's estate.

Lebowitz, Fran. Quoted in "Friendship, Fran Lebowitz Style," *Mirabella*, December 1992.

Lehmann, Rosamond. *The Echoing Grove*. Penguin, London, 1981. Used by permission of The Society of Authors, Literary representative of the Estate of Rosamond Lehmann.

Lerner, Harriet Goldhor. *The Dance of Anger: A Woman's Guide to Changing the Patterns of Intimate Relationships*. Harper & Row, New York, 1985. Copyright © 1985 by Harriet Goldhor Lerner. Reprinted by permission of HarperCollins Publishers.

Lessing, Doris. *The Summer Before the Dark*. Alfred A. Knopf, New York, 1973. Used by permission of Jonathan Cape and Random House, Inc.

Lifshin, Lyn, ed. *Ariadne's Thread: A Collection of Contemporary Women's Journals*. Harper & Row, New York, 1982.

Lindbergh, Anne Morrow. From *Gift from the Sea*, copyright © 1955 by Anne Morrow Lindbergh. Reprinted by permission of Pantheon Books, a division of Random House, Inc.

Mansfield, Katherine. *The Journal of Katherine Mansfield, 1904–1922*, Ed. J. Middleton Murray, Constable, London, 1962.

Marshall, Paule. *The Chosen Place, The Timeless People*. Harcourt, Brace and World, New York, 1969. Used by permission of the author.

Martineau, Harriet. *Harriet Martineau's Autobiography*. Virago, London, 1983.

Meigs, Mary. *Lily Briscoe: A Self-Portrait*. Talonbooks, Vancouver, 1981. Used by permission of the author.

Miller, Jean Baker. *Toward a New Psychology of Women*. Beacon Press, Boston, 1977. Used by permission of the author.

Moffat, Mary Jane, and Charlotte Painter, eds. *Revelations: Diaries of Women*. Vintage Books, New York, 1975. Used by permission of Random House, Inc.

Montague, Lady Mary Wortley. Quoted in *Between Ourselves, Letters Between Mothers and Daughters*, edited by Karen Payne. Houghton Mifflin Company, Boston, 1983.

Munro, Alice. From "Winter Wind" in *Something I've Been Meaning to Tell You*. McGraw-Hill, Ryerson, Toronto, 1974. Used by permission of the author.

Nin, Anaïs. *A Woman Speaks, The Lectures, Seminars and Interviews of Anaïs Nin*, ed. by Evelyn J. Hinz. The Swallow Press, Chicago, 1975. Used by permission of Gunther Stuhlmann, author's representative.

O'Brien, Edna. Excerpt from "The Love Object" from *A Fanatic Heart*. Copyright © 1984 by Edna O'Brien. Reprinted by permission of Farrar, Straus, and Giroux, Inc. and Wylie, Aitken and Stone, Inc.

Otto, Whitney. *How to Make An American Quilt*. Villard Books, New York, 1991. Used by permission of Random House, Inc.

Phelps, Elizabeth Stuart Lyon. *Story of Avis*. Quoted in *Silences* by Tillie Olsen, Delacorte Press, New York, 1978.

Praxilla. In *A Book of Women Poets*, ed. by Aliki Barnstone and Willis Barnstone. Schocken Books, New York, 1980.

Ptaschkina, Nellie. *Diary of Nellie Ptaschkina*, trans. by Pauline D. Chary. Jonathan Cape, London, 1923.

Richardson, Dorothy. *Pilgrimage, Vol. 1 and Vol. 4*. Alfred A. Knopf, New York, 1938. Used by permission of Mark Paterson on behalf of the Dorothy Richardson Estate.

Sarton, May. *A World of Light, Portraits and Celebrations*. W. W. Norton and Company, New York, 1976. Used by permission of W. W. Norton and Company.

Sevigne, Marquise de, Marie (de Rabutin Chantal). *Letters of Madame de Sevigne to Her Daughter and Her Friends*, selected, with an introductory essay by Richard Aldington. Brentano, New York, 1927.

Sexton, Anne. From "The Double Image" in *To Bedlam and Partway Back*. Copyright © 1960 by Anne Sexton. Reprinted by permission of Houghton Mifflin Company. All rights reserved.

Shelley, Mary W. *Frankenstein, or The Modern Prometheus*, ed. by James Rieger. Bobbs-Merrill, New York, 1974.

Spark, Muriel. *The Prime of Miss Jean Brodie*. Macmillan, London, 1961. Used by permission of David Higham Associates.

Spencer, Anna Garlin. *Woman's Share in Social Culture*. Arno Press, New York, 1912.

Steinem, Gloria. *Revolution from Within: A Book of Self-Esteem*. Little, Brown, Boston, 1992. Used by permission of Little, Brown and Company.

Swanwick, H. M. *The Future of The Women's Movement*. G. Bell and Sons, London, 1913.

Tan, Amy. *The Kitchen God's Wife*. G. P. Putnam's, New York, 1991. Reprinted by permission of The Putnam Publishing Group. Copyright © 1991 by Amy Tan.

Tolstoy, Sophie. *The Diary of Tolstoy's Wife, 1860–1891*. Trans. by Alexander Werth, London, Victor Gollancz Ltd., 1928.

Woolf, Virginia. Excerpt from *A Room of One's Own*. Copyright © 1929 by Harcourt, Brace, and Jovanovich, Inc. and renewed 1957 by Leonard Woolf. Reprinted by permission of Harcourt, Brace, and Jovanovich, The Hogarth Press, and the estate of the author.

Wordsworth, Dorothy. *Journals of Dorothy Wordsworth*, ed. by Mary Moorman. Oxford University Press, Oxford, England, 1971.

Worthington, Robin. *Thinking About Marriage*. The Abbey Press, St. Meinrad, Indiana, 1971. Used by permission of the publisher.